ACTIVITIES FOR MINECRAFTERS:
EARTH

Puzzles and Games for Hours of Fun!

Jen Funk Weber

Illustrations by Amanda Brack

Sky Pony Press
New York

Copyright © 2020 by Hollan Publishing, Inc.
Minecraft® is a registered trademark of Notch Development AB.

The Minecraft game is copyright © Mojang AB.

Sky Pony Press books may be purchased in bulk at special discounts for sales promotion, corporate gifts, fund-raising, or educational purposes. Special editions can also be created to specifications. For details, contact the Special Sales Department, Sky Pony Press, 307 West 36th Street, 11th Floor, New York, NY 10018 or info@skyhorsepublishing.com.

Sky Pony® is a registered trademark of Skyhorse Publishing, Inc.®, a Delaware corporation.

Minecraft® is a registered trademark of Notch Development AB.
The Minecraft game is copyright © Mojang AB.

Visit our website at www.skyponypress.com.

10 9 8 7 6 5 4 3 2 1

Cover design by Brian Peterson
Interior art by Amanda Brack
Puzzles created by Jen Funk Weber
Book design by Noora Cox

Print ISBN: 978-1-5107-6192-6

Printed in China

TABLE OF CONTENTS

HIDDEN TAPPABLES 1

An icon is tappable if it appears in all four boxes. Only two of the below items appear in every box. Can you find and circle the two tappables before they despawn?

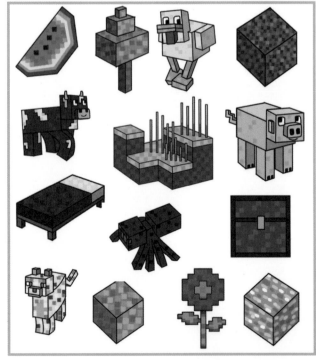

MOB DROPS

Four Minecraft Earth players collected special mob variants today. Follow the paths under and over crossing paths to discover which mob dropped into which player's inventory.

WOOLY COW   CLUCKSHROOM   JUMBO RABBIT   JOLLY LLAMA

TRISHENANIGAN   CL LOVES
                    STEFFEEFEE   JANA   GREEN
                                        BANANA

FUNNY FOOD

Build a crossword on this buildplate. Use the picture clues to guess the word answers, then figure out where each word logically fits. Transfer the numbered letters to the spaces with the same numbers. If you fill in the puzzle correctly, you'll get funny answers to the questions below.

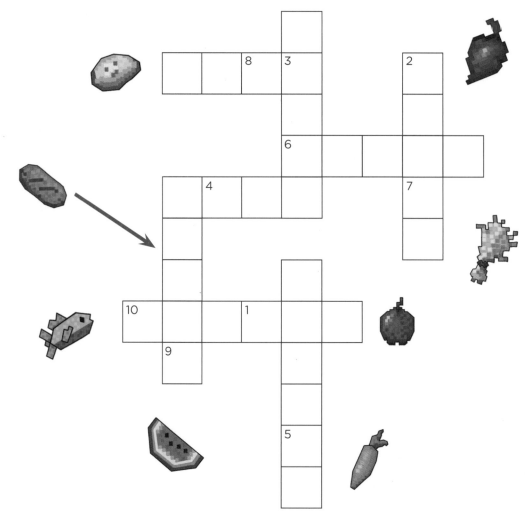

What Minecraft Earth vegetable is most angry?

$\overline{\quad}$ $\overline{\quad}$ $\overline{\quad}$ $\overline{\quad}$ $\overline{\quad}$ $\overline{\quad}$ $\overline{\quad}$ $\overline{\quad}$ $\overline{\quad}$ $\overline{\quad}$ $\overline{\quad}$ $\overline{\quad}$ $\overline{\quad}$ $\overline{\quad}$ $\overline{\quad}$ $\overline{\quad}$
 5   3   4   8   5   4   6   2   4   9   10   6   1   1   7   5

What Minecraft Earth vegetable is most highly regarded?

$\overline{\quad}$ $\overline{\quad}$ $\overline{\quad}$ $\overline{\quad}$ $\overline{\quad}$ $\overline{\quad}$ $\overline{\quad}$ $\overline{\quad}$ $\overline{\quad}$ $\overline{\quad}$ $\overline{\quad}$ $\overline{\quad}$ $\overline{\quad}$ $\overline{\quad}$ $\overline{\quad}$ $\overline{\quad}$ $\overline{\quad}$
 5   3   4   4   8   5   4   4   2   4   9   10   6   1   1   7   5

FREE FOR THE TAPPING

Read the three clues below to identify which of the nine items is tappable. Circle it and tap away!

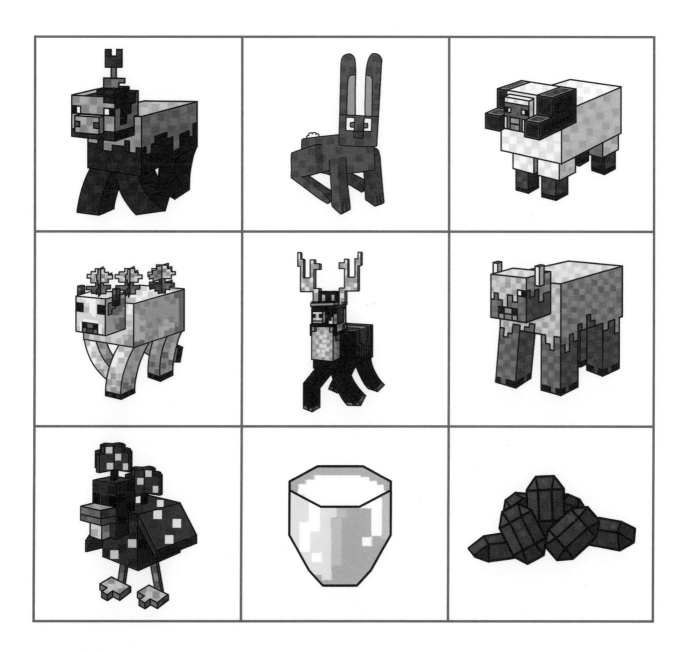

CLUES:

1. The tappable icon is either in the top row, the right column, or the center square.

2. The tappable icon is not in a corner square.

3. The tappable icon is not a woolly cow or a jolly llama.

CAPTURE THE MOOBLOOM

Warning: This maze will have you running around in circles like a Cluckshroom in direct sunlight! If you can avoid the creeper and get to the Moobloom, it's yours!

START

A JOLLY GOOD FRIEND

Get the hostile skeletons before they get you! Kill the right ones, and you can add a good joke to your inventory.

Here are the rules: Wipe out every skeleton above a llama, directly to the left of a sheep block, or below a chicken. Write letters from the remaining skeletons on the spaces to reveal the answer to the joke.

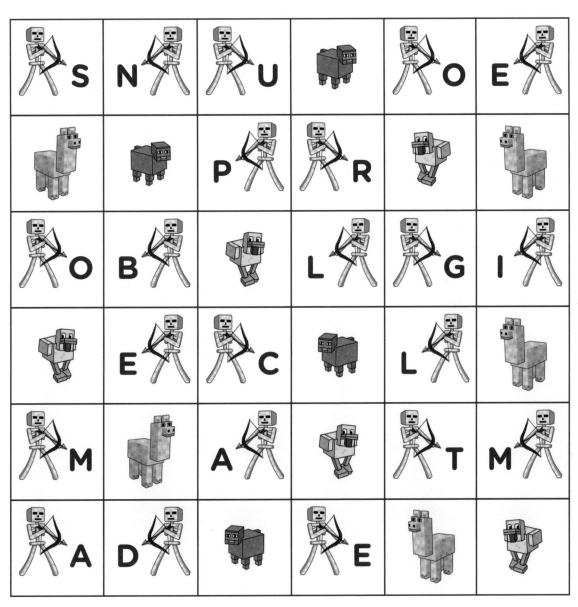

What does a Jolly Llama say when you ask him for a favor?

___ ___   ___   ___ ___ ___ ___ ___   ___ ___ ___ ___

TEAM BUILDING

Build the word wall on this buildplate by placing the 2x2 letter blocks in their proper places. If you place them correctly, you'll reveal the trick to Minecraft Earth team building. **Heads up:** Words are separated by black squares and wrap from one line to the next.

T	H	I	S	■	I	S
■	W	H	A	T	■	A
■	W	O	R	D	■	W
A	L	L	■	L	O	O
K	S	■	L	I	K	E

U	S	E			R	■	C			E	S
■	T	O			N	V	I			■	F
		E	N	D	S	■	T	O			U
		D	■	W	I	T	H	■			U

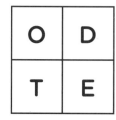

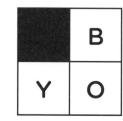

DANCE PARTY DISASTERS

Crack the code. Write the name of each icon on the spaces provided. Replace each number pair in the code with a letter in one of the icon names. For instance, 2-4 means the fourth letter in word #2 below.

1. _ _ _ _ _ _

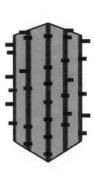

2. _ _ _ T _ _

3. _ _ _ _

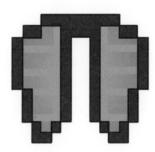

4. _ _ _ _ _ _ _

Why are wooly cows terrible dancers?

T _ _ _   _ _ _ _   _ _ _
2-4 1-2 4-1 4-3   1-2 4-6 1-4 4-1   4-4 3-1 1-3

_ _ _ _   _ _ _ _
3-3 4-1 3-4 4-4   3-4 1-5 4-1 2-4

ARROW ADVENTURE

To complete this maze adventure, you must follow the arrows. If you can find the path that leads from START to FINISH and avoids the creepers, you can claim ten rubies and lots of experience points! If there are two arrows in a square, you can choose to go either direction.

START   FINISH

MUDDY PIG
RUNNING AMOK

Can you catch the muddy pig? The word MUDDY PIG appears only once (forward or backward) in a horizontal, vertical, or diagonal line. If you find it, circle it!

D G I P Y M M U G P

U Y G D D U M M U M

M M I M M D U D M M

M U P M D Y D I U G

Y D Y Y P I G D D I

P P D D N M Y Y D Y

I M D G P P P D Y D

G M U D I I I D G D

M U M G P G G U I U

G U P Y D D U M P M

HIDDEN TAPPABLES II

An icon is tappable if it appears in all four boxes. Only two of the below items appear in every box. Can you find and circle the two tappables before they despawn?

GROUP ADVENTURE: FOUR FOR ORE

Four Minecraft Earth players are sharing an adventure in a local park, looking to mine some diamonds. Follow each player's path, under and over crossing paths, to discover who, if anyone, reaches the diamond ore.

HUSHED CROWD

Build a crossword on this buildplate. Use the picture clues to guess the word answers, then figure out where each word logically fits. Transfer the numbered letters to the spaces with the same numbers. If you fill in the puzzle correctly, you'll get a funny answer to the question below.

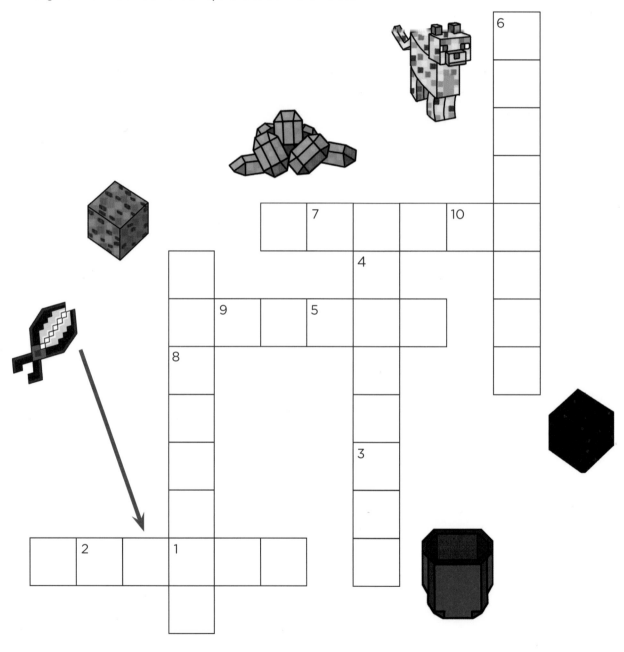

What do you call a room where chickens have to be quiet?

— — — — — — — — — — — — —
1   7   3   9   7   5   8   2   6   10   10   4

TRICKY TRICK KEY

The key to opening this chest is tapping one of the icons below. Follow the three clues below to decide which of the nine icons is tappable. Circle the icon when you figure it out, and tap away!

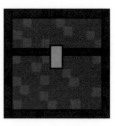

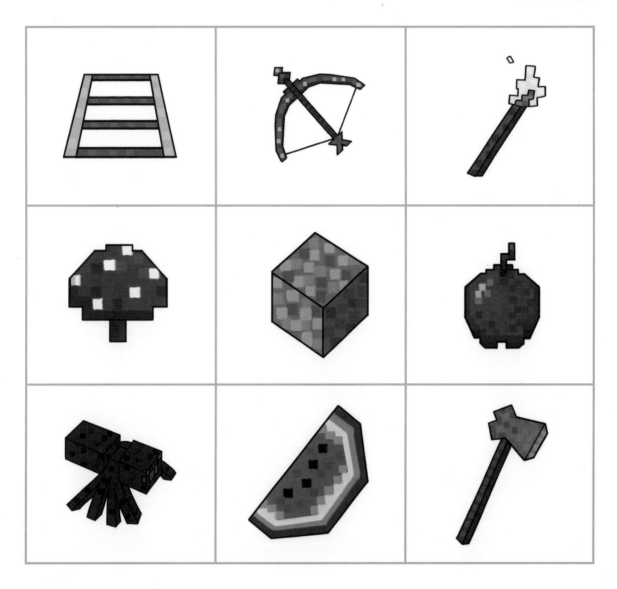

CLUES:

1. The tappable icon is either in a corner square or the middle row.

2. The tappable icon is not the torch or in line with the torch, vertically or horizontally.

3. The tappable icon is not mined or planted.

BEACON BOUND

There's a Minecraft Earth adventure beacon on your screen. You're armed and ready to battle mobs, mine, and search for treasure. Can you find your way through these crazy city streets to reach the adventure?

START

FINISH

PASSED OVER PASSIVE MOB

Cross off every mob above a block of grass, to the right of a tree, and between two diagonal red mushrooms. Write letters from the remaining mobs on the spaces to answer the riddle.

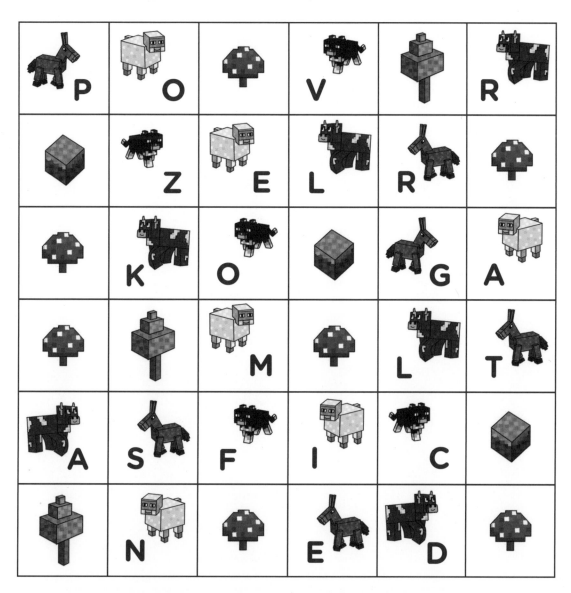

What peaceful animal was passed over as a passive mob for Minecraft Earth?

We can't tell you, but here's a hint:

Game developers thought it was _____ .

___ ___ ___ ___ ___ – ___ ___ ___ ___ ___ – ___ ___ ___ ___

REWARDING ADVICE

Build the word wall on this buildplate by placing the 2x2 letter blocks in their proper places. If you place them correctly, you'll reveal a tip for maximizing your Minecraft Earth resource gathering. **Heads up:** Words are separated by black squares and wrap from one line to the next.

Example grid:

T	H	I	S	■	■	I	S
■	W	H	A	T	■		A
■	W	O	R	D	■		W
A	L	L	■	■	L	O	O
K	S	■	■	L	I	K	E

Main grid:

D	O	■	C			L	L
E			E			T	H
E			R	E	W		
D	■		Y	O	U	■	
R	■	T	H			G	S
■	Y	O	U			P	R
O			B	L	Y	■	D
O			N	Y	W	A	Y

Letter blocks:

| H | A |
| S. | ■ |

| A | R |
| F | O |

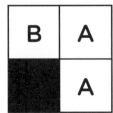

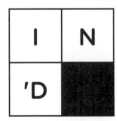

HEAR THIS!

Write the name of each Minecraft Earth item on the spaces. Solve the riddle by replacing each number pair in the code with a letter in one of the icon names. For instance, 1-4 means the fourth letter in the first word below.

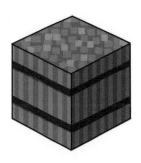

1. __ __ __ __

__ __ __ __ __

2. __ __ __

__ __ __ __

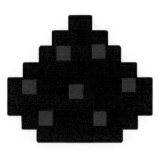

3. __ __ __ __ __ __

4. __ __ __ __ __ __ __

__ __ __ __

What are the loudest animals in Minecraft Earth?

__ __ __   __ __ __ __ __ __
1-9 2-1 3-5   2-1 4-6 3-6 1-6 4-8 1-4

__ __ __ __ __
3-1 2-1 2-7 4-8 3-2

NAVIGATIONAL HAZARDS

There are mobs to be fought and gems to be mined on the other side of this maze! Follow the arrows to complete the Minecraft Earth adventure. If there are two arrows in a box, you can choose to go either direction. Can you avoid the lava and get out in fighting condition?

START **FINISH**

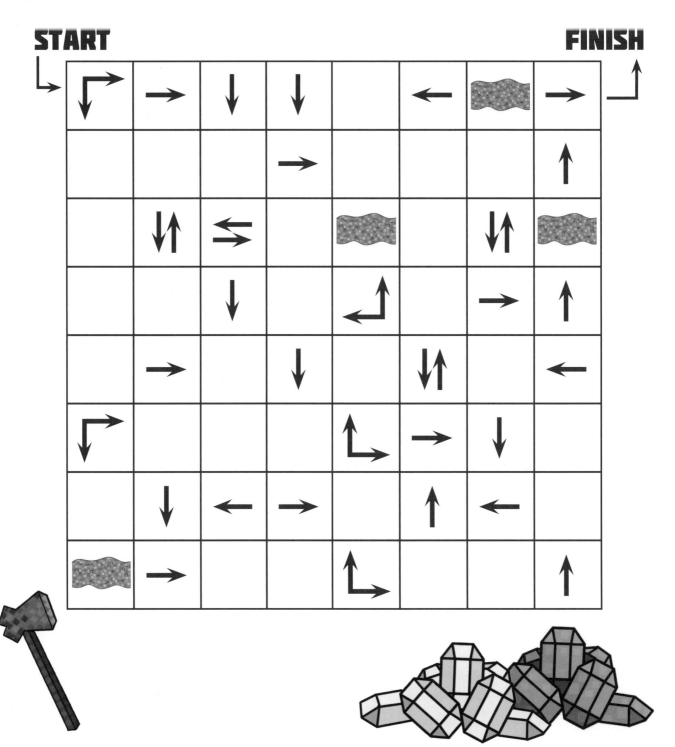

EPIC HUNT

Find and circle the names of 12 epic and rare drops in the word search. They might be forward, backward, up, down, or diagonal. Write unused letters on the blank spaces in order from top to bottom and left to right to discover something useful to know.

Hint: Circle individual letters instead of whole words to better isolate remaining letters. We've found one to get you started.

M	D	U	S	P	I	L	U	T	D	P	D
Y	P	U	I	R	O	O	D	N	O	R	I
G	R	S	M	A	R	G	E	W	E	P	P
I	C	E	D	F	R	R	E	O	P	U	V
K	S	F	T	A	O	R	R	O	M	C	I
P	C	I	N	A	E	T	G	T	A	R	N
Y	S	I	A	D	E	Y	E	X	O	E	E
P	T	P	R	A	B	P	L	K	E	T	S
E	S	A	T	B	A	P	E	A	C	T	W
A	I	S	R	A	B	N	O	R	I	U	Y
Ⓛ	Ⓐ	Ⓥ	Ⓐ	Ⓑ	Ⓤ	Ⓒ	Ⓚ	Ⓔ	Ⓣ	B	B

BRICK

BUCKET OF MUD

BUTTERCUP

GRANITE

IRON BARS

IRON DOOR

~~LAVA BUCKET~~

OXEYE DAISY

POWERED RAIL

REPEATER

TULIPS

VINES

_ _ _ _ _ _   _ _ _ _ _   _ _   _ _

_ _ _ _ _   _ _ _ _   _ _ _ _ _

_ _ _ _ _ _ _ _ _ _ _ .   _ _ _ _   _ _ _ _ _ !

HIDDEN TAPPABLES III

Two of the items in the boxes below are tappables. An icon is tappable if it appears in all four boxes. Can you find and circle the two tappables before they despawn?

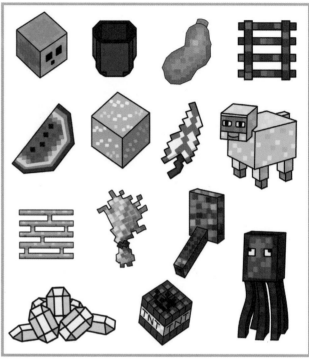

LLAMA DRAMA

Four players are racing to claim the Jolly Llama for their Minecraft Earth inventories. Follow each player's path under and over crossing paths to discover who finds the holiday-themed llama variant.

BUILT TO LAST

Use the picture clues to guess the word answers, then figure out where each word logically fits. Transfer the numbered letters to the spaces with the same numbers to answer the riddle.

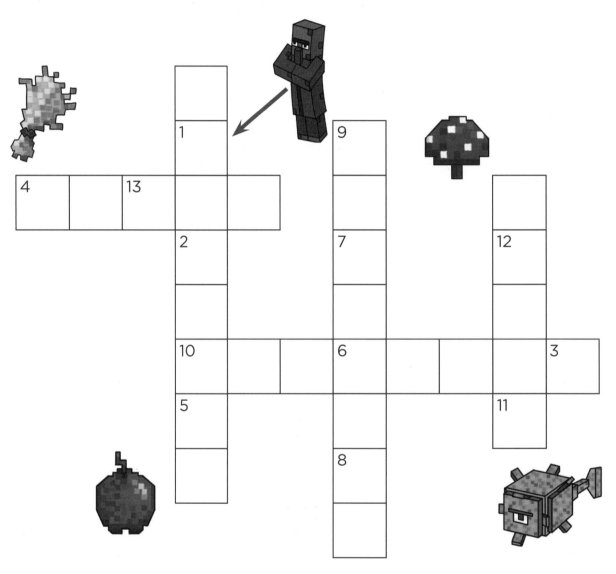

To make something you build last so that others can enjoy it, turn it into this:

$\overline{4}$ $\overline{13}$ $\overline{5}$ $\overline{6}$ $\overline{7}$ $\overline{1}$ $\overline{7}$ $\overline{11}$ $\overline{5}$ $\overline{3}$ $\overline{11}$

$\overline{12}$ $\overline{8}$ $\overline{2}$ $\overline{8}$ $\overline{10}$ $\overline{6}$ $\overline{4}$ $\overline{9}$

SECRET SPELUNKING ENTRANCE

Who's up for some spelunking? To enter the cave and start this Minecraft Earth puzzle adventure, you must tap one of the icons below. Follow the clues and circle the icon that is tappable.

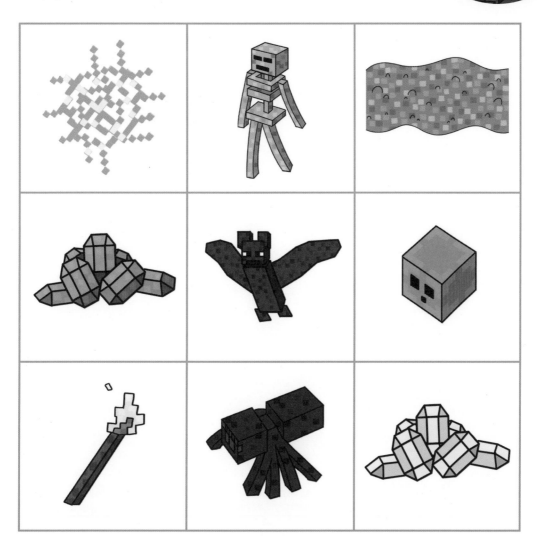

CLUES:

1. The tappable icon is either a gem or a mob.

2. The tappable icon is either in the top row or the center column, but not both.

3. The tappable icon is never hostile.

RUBY QUEST

Find your way through this maze from Start to the Ruby treasure. *Cha-ching!*

START

MOST SPECIAL MOB

Cross out and destroy every hostile mob to the right of a block. Then cross out mobs between two flowers horizontally or vertically (not diagonally). Write letters from the remaining mobs on the spaces to reveal the answer to this question:

What was the rarest mob to drop from a tappable chest in the early days of Minecraft Earth?

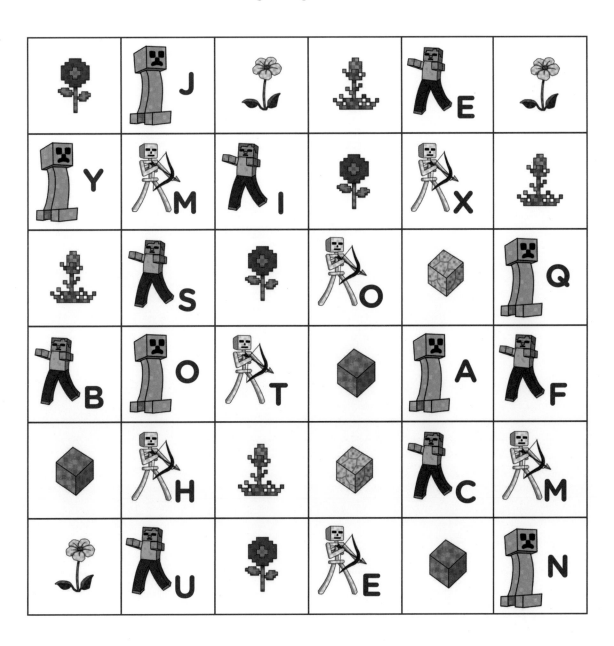

_____ _____ _____ _____   _____ _____ _____

DISASTER WARNING

Build the word wall on this buildplate by placing the 2x2 letter blocks in their proper places. If you place them correctly, you'll reveal a tip that might help prevent a disaster. **Heads up:** Words are separated by black squares and wrap from one line to the next.

T	H	I	S	■	I	S
■	W	H	A	T	■	A
■	W	O	R	D	■	W
A	L	L	■	L	O	O
K	S	■	L	I	K	E

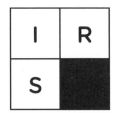

A	N
E	R

I	O
E	■

I	R
S	■

E	R
S	■

I	N
A	R

P	R
T	E

F			E	■	S			E	A
D			F	A	S			R	■
I	N	■	M			E	C	R	A
F	T	■	E			T	H	■	T
H		■		O	T	H			■
V		■	S			N			O
F	■	T	H			G	A	M	E

PUNNY BUSINESS

Write the name of each icon on the spaces. Replace each number pair in the code with a letter in one of the icon names to solve the riddle. For instance, 1-4 means the fourth letter in the first word below.

1. __ __ __ __ __ __

2. __ __ __ __ __ __

__ __ __ __

3. __ __ __ __ __

4. __ __ __ __ __

__ __ __

**What did the cobblestone block say
to the Minecraft Earth player?**

'

___ ___ ___ ___   ___ ___ ___ ___   ___ ___
4-4   1-3   2-6   2-3   2-4   3-1   1-4   2-9   4-1   1-6

___ ___ ___   ___ ___ ___ ___ ___ ___ ___
2-7   3-4   3-2   4-8   3-3   3-1   2-6   1-5   2-4   2-5

STUCK!

Can you find your way out of this desert maze without getting stuck? (On a cactus, that is.) Move in the direction an arrow points until you come to a new sign. If there are two arrows in a box, you can choose to go either direction. Can you go find the path that leads from START to FINISH and avoids the cacti?

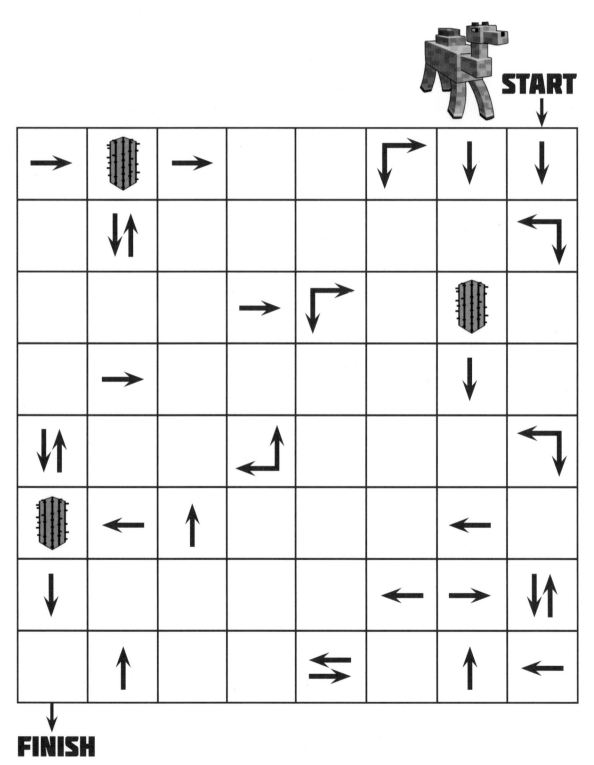

START

FINISH

A RARE DROP

Can you find the word MOOBLOOM in the letters below to get it to drop into your inventory? It appears only once in a horizontal, vertical, or diagonal line.

M M O O B L O M O O

O O M L O B O O M B

M M O O O B L O O M

B O L M O M L O B O

M M O O L B M L L O

B O L L O O O B O L

L B B O B O O O O B

O M M L M O M B M O

O M O O L B O M O M

M O O L O B O M M L

HIDDEN TAPPABLES IV

Two of the items in the boxes below are tappables. An icon is tappable if it appears in all four boxes. Can you find and circle the two tappables before they despawn?

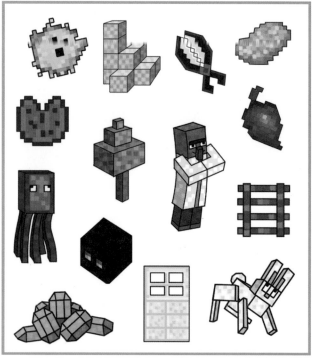

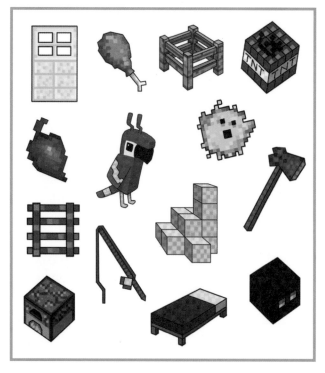

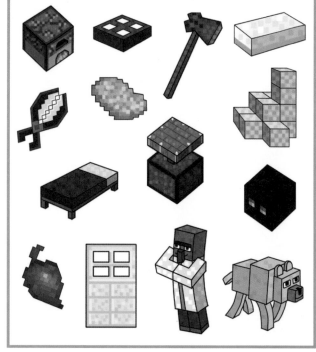

ARCTIC ADVENTURE

You invited four Minecraft Earth friends on an arctic adventure. Follow each friend's path, under and over crossing paths, to discover which friends joined you in the arctic.

MINDY   MAX   MIA   MILTON

OCELOTS RULE

Build a crossword on this buildplate. Use the picture clues to guess the word answers, then figure out where each word logically fits. Transfer the numbered letters to the spaces with the same numbers. If you fill in the puzzle correctly, you'll reveal the answer to the joke.

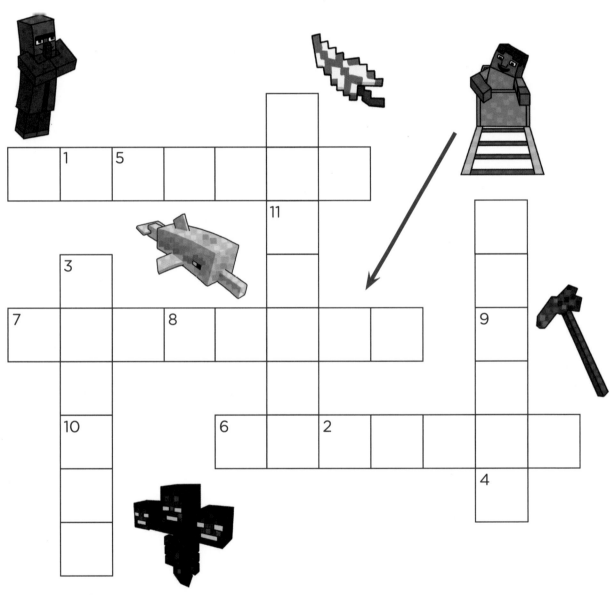

What do you call a group of ocelots that keep the peace in Minecraft Earth?

—— —— —— ——   —— —— —— —— —— —— —— —— —— —— ——
11 5   2   10   8   3   6   1   4   11 8   7   8   3   9

ON YOUR MARK, GET SET, TAP, GO!

One of your clever Minecraft Earth friends has built a cool redstone chain reaction device. To start it, you have to tap one of the icons in the grid. If you tap the wrong icon, the device locks. Use the clues to figure out which item needs to be tapped, and circle it to start the chain reaction.

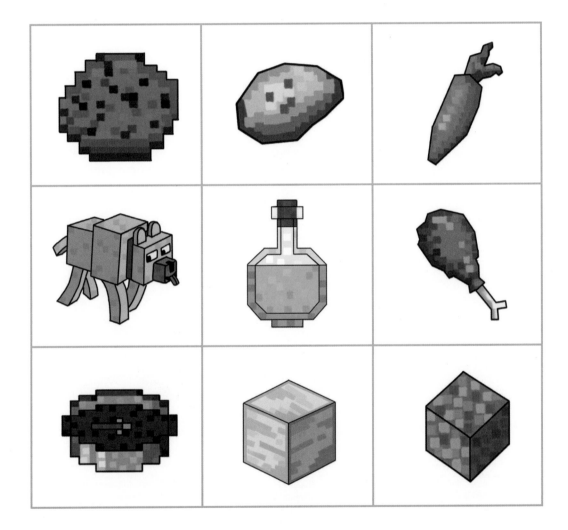

CLUES:

1. The tappable item is either a good building tool or a pet.

2. The tappable icon is directly below something edible.

3. The tappable icon is either in the bottom row or the center column.

ROUND 'EM UP!

Catch these exclusive Minecraft Earth farm mobs as you find your way through this maze from START to FINISH.

START   **FINISH**

MOUNTAIN MERRIMENT

Cross out every llama to the left of or below a silverfish. Then cross out every llama to the right of or above emeralds. Write letters from the remaining llamas on the spaces to fill in the blanks and answer the joke.

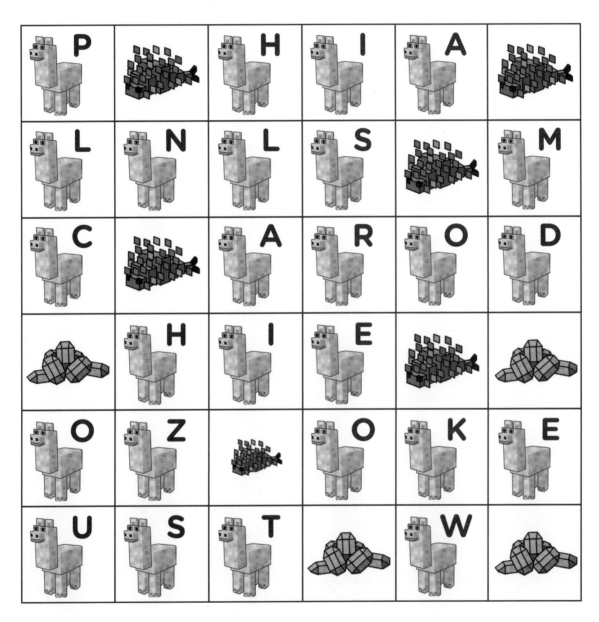

Why can't you wander through mountain biomes without laughing your head off?

Because they're _____.

—

___ ___ ___ ___ ___   ___ ___ ___ ___ ___ ___

TIP FOR TAPS

Here's a tip we all can use: To find out what it is, build the word wall on this buildplate by placing the 2x2 letter blocks in their proper places. If you place them correctly, you'll reveal a tip that unlocks more Minecraft Earth fun. **Heads up:** Words are separated by black squares and wrap from one line to the next.

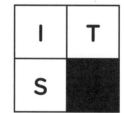

T	H	I	S		I	S
	W	H	A	T		A
	W	O	R	D		W
A	L	L			L	O
K	S			L	I	K
						E

E	L
L	O

A	N
U	I

I	T
S	

R	I
S	

N	
	P

A	P
L	E

E	A	R			E	X	P	E			E
N	C	E			O	I	N	T			W
		H		T			P	A	B	L	E
		T	O				V				U
P				D		U	N			C	K
	B			L	D	P	L	A	T	E	S

WORD TO THE WISE

Crack the code for a handy piece of advice about buildplates in Minecraft Earth. Write the name of each icon on the spaces. Replace each number pair in the code with a letter in one of the icon names. For instance, 1-4 is the fourth letter in the first word below.

1. __ __ __ __ __ __ __ __ __

3. __ __ __ __ __ __

2. __ __ __ __ __ __ __

__ __ __ __

4. __ __ __ __ __

__ __ __ __ __ __

Before you invite friends to build with you, consider this:

__ __ __ __ __ __ __ __ __ __ __   __ __ __
3-1 1-3 4-4 4-10 1-1 4-3 4-1 3-3 1-6 3-2 2-3   3-4 4-7 2-6

__ __   __ __ __ __ __ __ __
3-1 3-2   2-7 1-2 4-11 3-2 2-1 3-2 1-1

KABOOM!

Can you find your way through this dangerous maze without running into TNT? Move in the direction an arrow points until you come to a new sign. If there are two arrows in a box, you can choose to go either direction.

START **FINISH**

ATTENTION, EARTH THINGS

Can you find all the Minecraft Earth things in the word search? They might be forward, backward, up, down, or diagonal. Write unused letters on the blank spaces, in order from top to bottom and left to right to discover something useful to know.

Hint: Circle individual letters instead of whole words to better isolate remaining letters. We've found one to get you started.

I **W O O L Y C O W** M F
Y A M A L L Y L L O J
M O E U S H E M A O B
R O A M M O U O T R E
B L O O F D O A M H A
B U I L D O P Y O S C
U W I Y B P B L L K O
G E P T A O A O B C N
T I B B A R O B M U J
G U L T T E R M C L U
T E K C U B D U M C P

BEACON
BUILD
CLUCKSHROOM
JOLLY LLAMA
JUMBO RABBIT
MOB OF ME
MOOBLOOM
MUD BUCKET
MUDDY PIG
TAPPABLE
~~**WOOLY COW**~~

__ __   __ __ __   __ __ __ __ __   __

__ __ __ __ __ __ __ __ __ __ __ , __ __ __   __ __ __ __

__ __ __ __   __   __ __ __ __ __ __ __ __ .

HIDDEN TAPPABLES V

Two of the items in the boxes below are tappables. An icon is tappable if it appears in all four boxes. Can you find and circle the two tappables before they despawn?

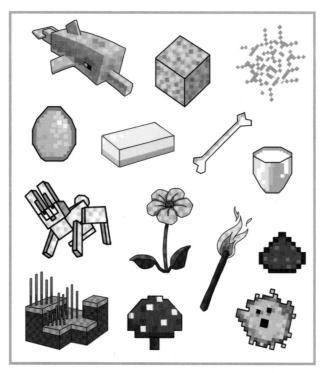

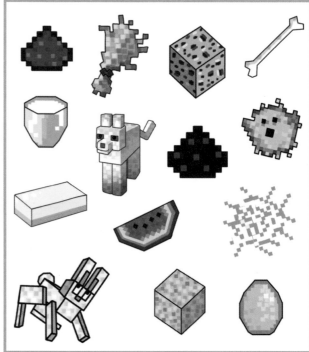

QR QUEST

A life-sized statue of a moobloom was placed in a local park. Six friends hope to reach it, click the QR code, and receive a special, secret drop. Follow each player's path, under and over crossing paths, to discover which players, if any, find the life-sized moobloom.

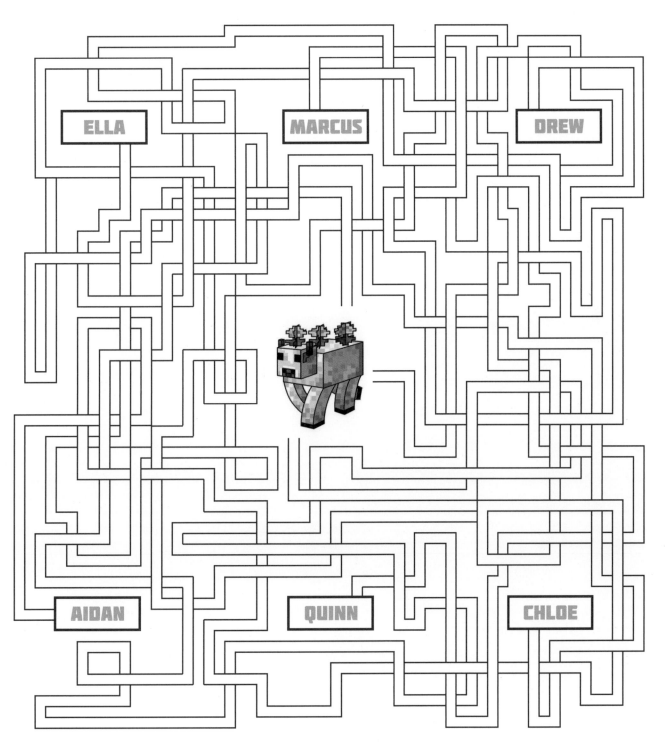

THE NAME OF THE GAME

Build a crossword on this buildplate. Use the picture clues to guess the word answers, then figure out where each word logically fits. Transfer the numbered letters to the spaces with the same numbers to answer the riddle.

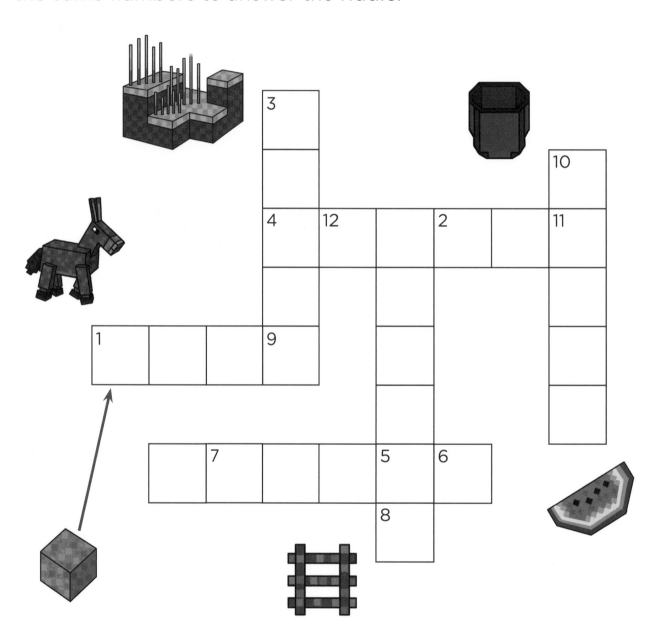

What kind of game is Minecraft Earth?

___ ___ ___ ___ ___ ___ ___ ___ ___   ___ ___ ___ ___ ___ ___ ___
12 7 10 3 5 9 6 5 2   11 5 12 4 1 6 8

CEASE FIRE!

Escape hostile mobs by using the clues to discover which one of the icons below is tappable. If you tap the wrong icon, you're on your own with the mobs. If you tap the right icon, they will all despawn. Circle the icon that is tappable.

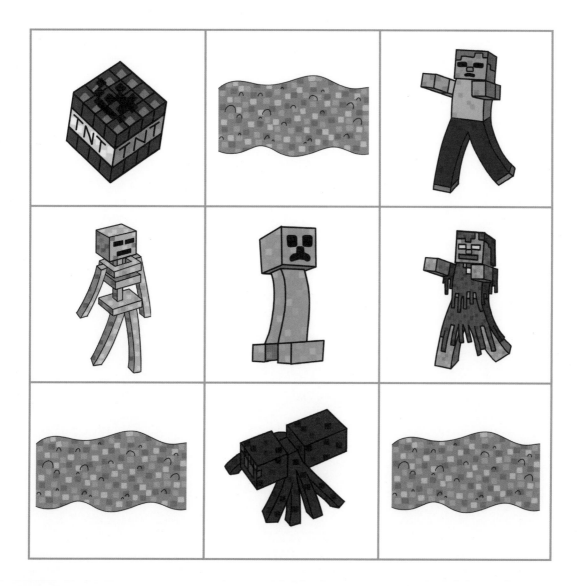

CLUES:

1. The tappable icon is either in the middle row or a corner square.

2. The tappable icon is a mob.

3. The tappable icon is to the right of a lava river.

TAP AND GO

You've located a tappable pink sheep, but two skeletons roam nearby. Make your way to the sheep without coming into contact with the skeletons or their sharp arrows.

START   **FINISH**

A SLIPPERY SLOPE

Two Minecraft Earth resources are best kept separate. To find out what they are, write the name of each icon on the spaces. Replace each number pair in the code with a letter in one of the icon names. For instance, 1-4 is the fourth letter in the first word below.

1. ___ ___ ___ ___ ___

2. ___ ___ ___ ___ ___ ___ ___

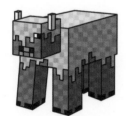

3. ___ ___ ___ ___ ___

4. ___ ___ ___ ___ ___ ___ ___

___ ___ ___

___ ___ ___ ___ ___   ___ ___ ___
3-1   4-3   2-3   1-5   2-7   3-7   4-3   1-3

___ ___ ___ ___ ___ ___ ___   ___   ___ ___ ___
4-7   2-6   4-8   2-3   2-7   3-3   1-6   4-3   4-4   2-2   1-1

___ ___ ___ ___ ___ ___   ___ ___ ___ ___ ___
4-8   3-8   2-2   2-7   2-4   1-5   2-1   3-4   1-2   3-7   1-4

OCEAN ADVENTURE

There's a shipwreck not too far off the beach in this Minecraft Earth adventure. If you can get there, you'll find good loot. Move in the direction an arrow points until you come to a new sign. If there are two arrows in a box, you can choose to go either direction. Can you find your way to the wreck without running into a drowned?

FINISH

START

CAMOUFLAGED COW

Can you find the letters of the word WOOLY COW in the puzzle below? It appears only once in a horizontal, vertical, or diagonal line.

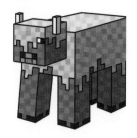

W O C L L O W O O L Y

O W O C W L O O W Y W

L Y C O W Y L O O W O

L W O O Y C O W O C W

Y L Y L O L O L Y O L

Y C Y L Y C Y L O O W

C W O C O C Y L O O W

O O O W O Y O L L Y O

W W O W C W L O W O C

W O C Y O L O O W O O

C L W O O Y L C O W L

HIDDEN TAPPABLES VI

Two of the items in the boxes below are tappables. An icon is tappable if it appears in all four boxes. Can you find and circle the two tappables before they despawn?

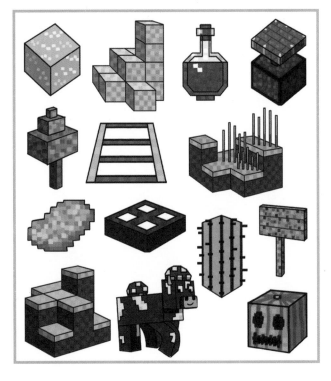

FINDERS KEEPERS

Four Minecraft Earth friends are about to be rewarded for adventuring. Follow each player's path, under and over crossing paths, to discover who gets what.

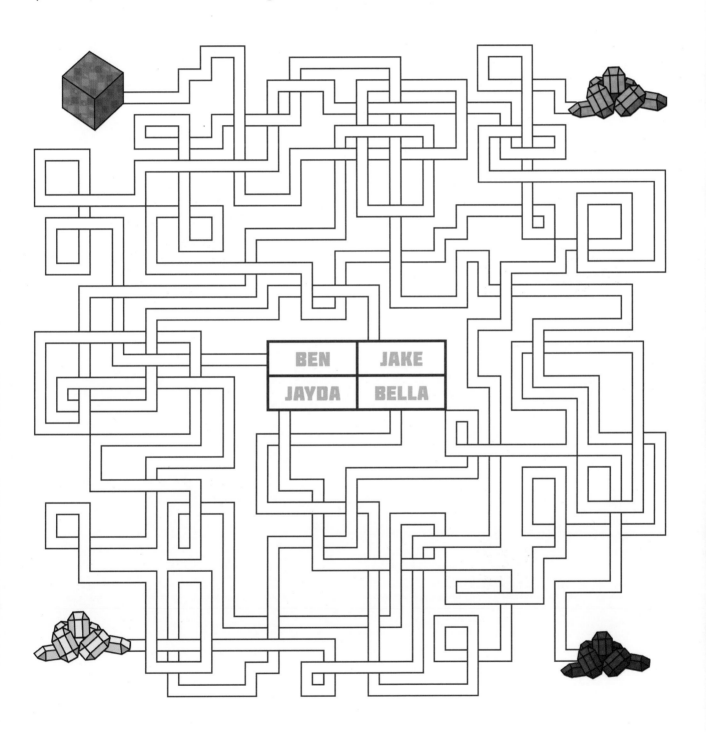

COOKING UP CLUES

Use the picture clues to guess the word answers, then figure out where each word logically fits. Transfer the numbered letters to the spaces with the same numbers. If you fill in the puzzle correctly, you'll discover a fun fact about adventures.

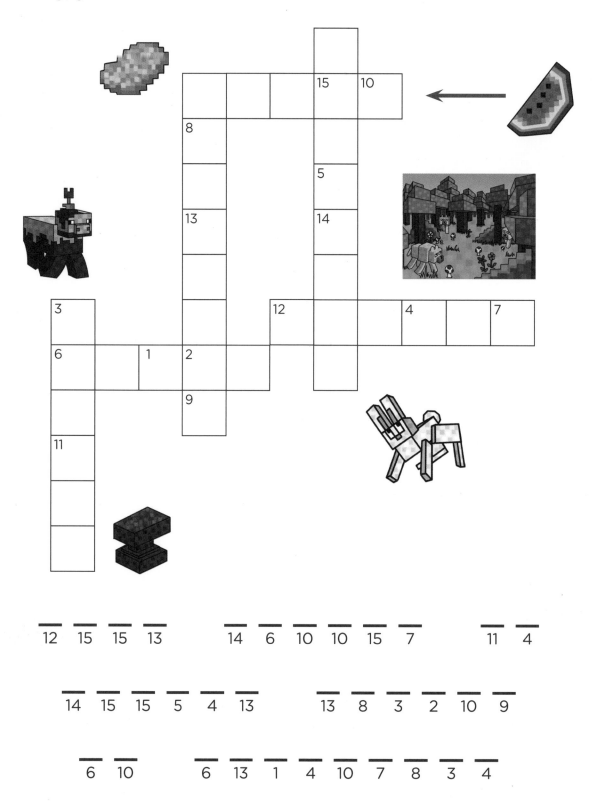

___ ___ ___ ___   ___ ___ ___ ___ ___ ___   ___ ___
12 15 15 13   14 6   10 10 15 7   11 4

___ ___ ___ ___ ___ ___   ___ ___ ___ ___ ___ ___
14 15 15 5   4   13   13 8   3   2   10 9

___ ___   ___ ___ ___ ___ ___ ___ ___ ___ ___
6   10   6   13 1   4   10 7   8   3   4

54

TRUE FRIENDS

Your friends are waiting to play Minecraft Earth with you on the other side of this maze. Can you find your way from START to FINISH? It will be easier if you correctly identify each statement as true or false.

START

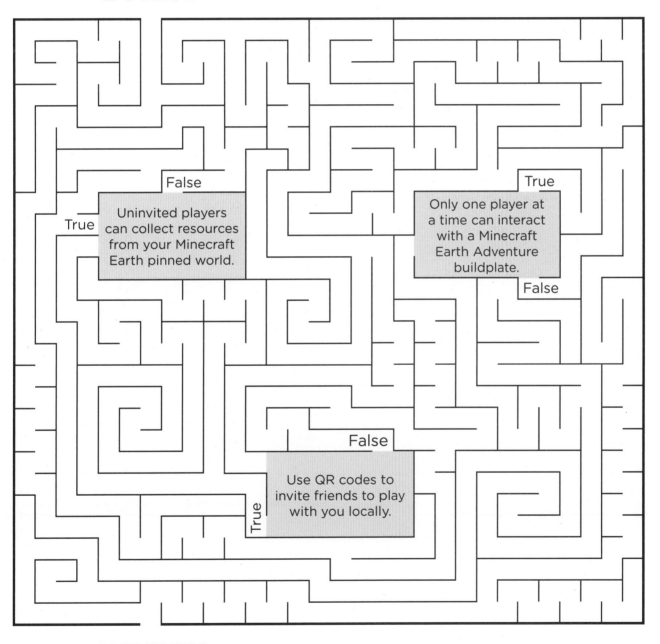

False

True

Uninvited players can collect resources from your Minecraft Earth pinned world.

True

Only one player at a time can interact with a Minecraft Earth Adventure buildplate.

False

False

True

Use QR codes to invite friends to play with you locally.

FINISH

ANSWER KEY

HIDDEN TAPPABLES I (Page 4)

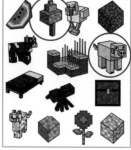

MOB DROPS (Page 5)

Wooly Cow - Trishenanigan
Cluckshroom - CL Loves Green
Jumbo Rabbit - Steffeefee
Jolly Llama - Jana Banana

FUNNY FOOD (Page 6)

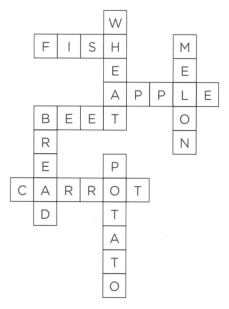

What Minecraft Earth vegetable is most angry? THE STEAMED CARROT

What Minecraft Earth vegetable is most highly regarded?
THE ESTEEMED CARROT

FREE FOR THE TAPPING (Page 7)

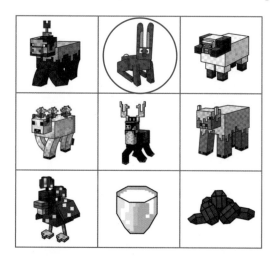

CAPTURE THE MOOBLOOM (Page 8)

START

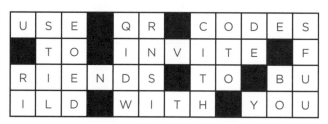

A JOLLY GOOD FRIEND (Page 9)

What does a Jolly Llama say when you ask him for a favor? NO PROB-LLAMA!

TEAM BUILDING (Page 10)

U	S	E	■	Q	R	■	C	O	D	E	S
■	T	O	■	I	N	V	I	T	E	■	F
R	I	E	N	D	S	■	T	O	■	B	U
I	L	D	■	W	I	T	H	■	Y	O	U

DANCE PARTY DISASTERS
(Page 11)

1. SHOVEL
2. CACTUS
3. WOLF
4. ELYTRA

Why are wooly cows terrible dancers?
THEY HAVE TWO LEFT FEET!

ARROW ADVENTURE (Page 12)

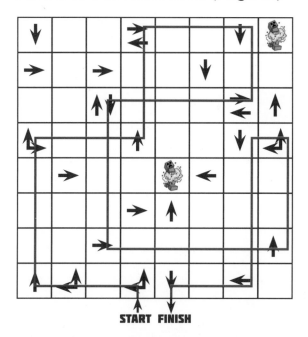

START FINISH

MUDDY PIG RUNNING AMOK
(Page 13)

HIDDEN TAPPABLES II (Page 14)

GROUP ADVENTURE: FOUR FOR ORE (Page 15)

Min and Phillipe reach the ore to mine diamonds.

HUSHED CROWD (Page 16)

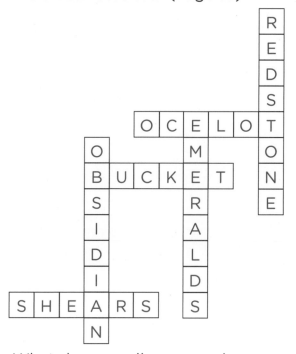

What do you call a room where chickens have to be quiet?

A CLUCKSHROOM
(A cluck shhhh room. Get it?)

TRICKY TRICK KEY (Page 17)

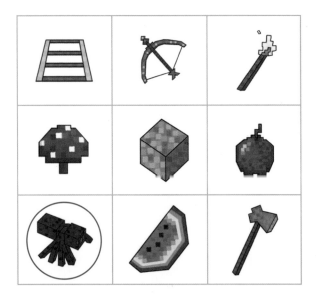

BEACON BOUND (Page 18)

START

FINISH

PASSED OVER PASSIVE MOB (Page 19)

What peaceful animal was passed over as a passive mob for Minecraft Earth? We can't tell you, but here's a hint: Game developers thought the animal was _____.

OVER-KOALA-FIED
(Yeah, that's a joke.)

REWARDING ADVICE (Page 20)

D	O			C	H	A	L	L
E	N	G	E	S.			T	H
E	Y			R	E	W	A	R
D			Y	O	U		F	O
R		T	H	I	N	G	S	
		Y	O	U	'D		P	R
O	B	A	B	L	Y			D
O		A	N	Y	W	A	Y	

HEAR THIS! (Page 21)

1. GOLD INGOT
2. HAY BALE
3. SPIDER
4. REDSTONE DUST

What is the loudest animal in Minecraft Earth?

THE HORNED SHEEP

NAVIGATIONAL HAZARDS
(Page 22)

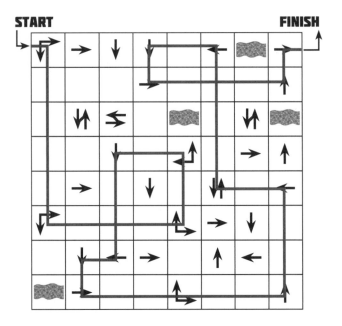

START FINISH

EPIC HUNT (Page 23)

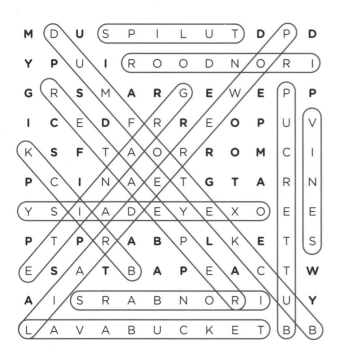

Muddy pigs are epic drops from pig tappables. Tap away!

HIDDEN TAPPABLES III (Page 24)

LLAMA DRAMA (Page 25)

Only M-Earth Gal gets to claim the Jolly Llama.

BUILT TO LAST (Page 26)

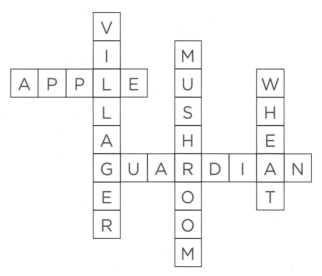

To make something you build last so that others can enjoy it, turn it into this:

A PERSISTENT HOLOGRAM

SECRET SPELUNKING ENTRANCE (Page 27)

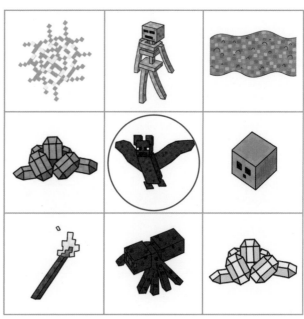

RUBY QUEST (Page 28)

START

MOST SPECIAL MOB (Page 29)

MOB OF ME
Of course you're the most special
mob in Minecraft Earth!

DISASTER WARNING (Page 30)

F	I	R	E			S	P	R	E	A
D	S		F	A	S	T	E	R		
I	N		M	I	N	E	C	R	A	
F	T		E	A	R	T	H			T
H	A	N			O	T	H	E	R	
V	E	R	S	I	O	N	S			O
F		T	H	E			G	A	M	E

PUNNY BUSINESS (Page 31)

1. COOKIE

2. ROTTEN FLESH

3. ARROW

4. MUDDY PIG

What did the cobblestone block say
to the Minecraft Earth player?

DON'T TAKE ME FOR GRANITE

STUCK! (Page 32)

START

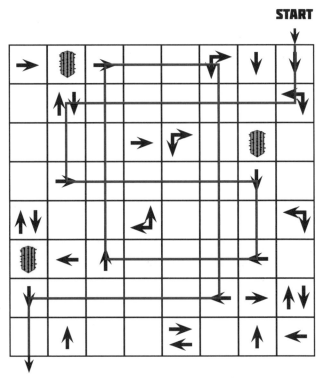

FINISH

A RARE DROP (Page 33)

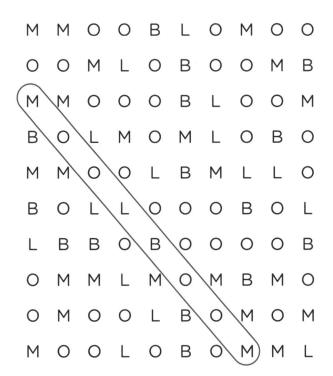

M M O O B L O M O O
O O M L O B O O M B
M M O O O B L O O M
B O L M O M L O B O
M M O O L B M L L O
B O L L O O O B O L
L B B O B O O O O B
O M M L M O M B M O
O M O O L B O M O M
M O O L O B O M M L

HIDDEN TAPPABLES IV (Page 34)

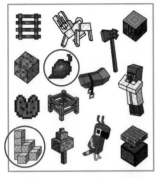
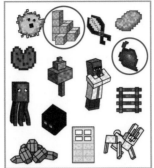
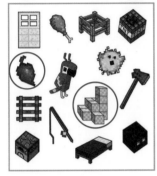
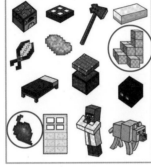

ON YOUR MARK, GET SET, TAP, GO! (Page 37)

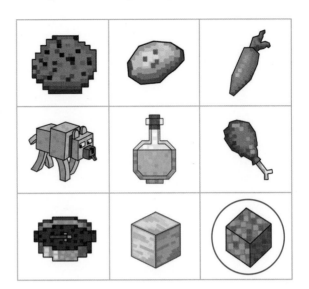

ARCTIC ADVENTURE (Page 35)

Mindy, Mia, and Milton join Matthew for the Adventure. Max does not.

OCELOTS RULE (Page 36)

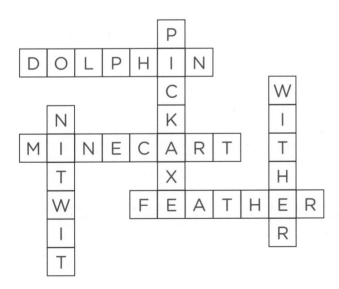

What do you call a group of ocelots that keep the peace in Minecraft Earth?

CLAW ENFORCEMENT

ROUND 'EM UP! (Page 38)

START   FINISH

MOUNTAIN MERRIMENT (Page 39)

Why can't you wander through mountain biomes without laughing your head off? Because they're

HILL-ARIOUS

61

TIP FOR TAPS (Page 40)

E	A	R	N		E	X	P	E	R	I	E
N	C	E		P	O	I	N	T	S		W
I	T	H		T	A	P	P	A	B	L	E
S		T	O		L	E	V	E	L		U
P		A	N	D		U	N	L	O	C	K
	B	U	I	L	D	P	L	A	T	E	S

WORD TO THE WISE (Page 41)

1. DRUMSTICK
2. FISHING POLE
3. BEACON
4. LAPIS LAZULI

BUILDPLATES CAN BE GRIEFED
So invite friends you trust.

KABOOM! (Page 42)

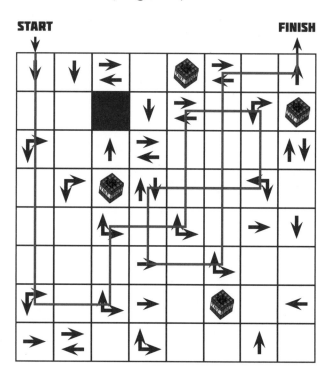

ATTENTION, EARTH THINGS
(Page 43)

IF YOU SHEAR A MOOBLOOM,
YOU WILL GET A BUTTERCUP.

HIDDEN TAPPABLES V (Page 44)

QR QUEST (Page 45)

Ella is the only player to reach the life-sized moobloom statue.

THE NAME OF THE GAME
(Page 46)

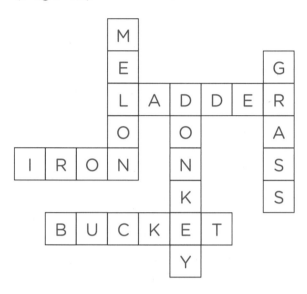

What kind of game is Minecraft Earth?

AUGMENTED REALITY

CEASE FIRE! (Page 47)

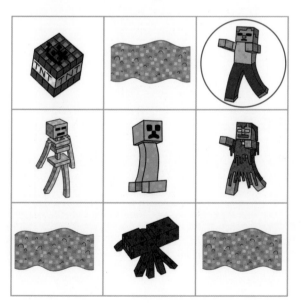

TAP AND GO (Page 48)

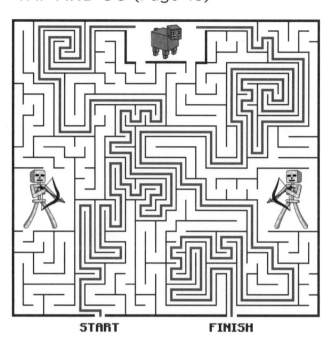

START   FINISH

A SLIPPERY SLOPE (Page 49)

1. DONKEY

2. BUTCHER

3. WOOLLY COW

4. DIAMONDS

WATER CAN DESTROY A MUD SOURCE BLOCK

OCEAN ADVENTURE (Page 50)

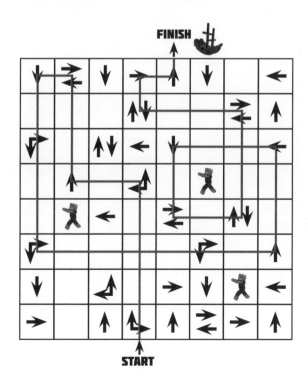

CAMOUFLAGED COW (Page 51)

```
W O C L L O W O O L Y
O W O C W L O O W Y W
L Y C O W Y L O O W O
L W O O Y C O W O C W
Y L Y L O L O L Y O L
Y C Y L Y C Y L O O W
C W O C O C Y L O O W
O O O W O Y O L L Y O
W W O W C W L O W O C
W O C Y O L O O W O O
C L W O O Y L C O W L
```

COOKING UP CLUES (Page 54)

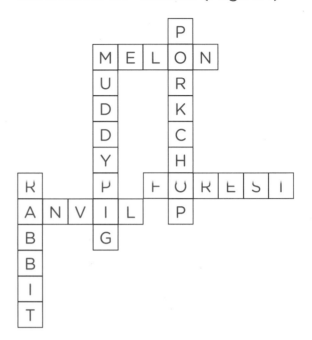

FOOD CANNOT BE COOKED
DURING AN ADVENTURE

HIDDEN TAPPABLES VI (Page 52)

TRUE FRIENDS (Page 55)

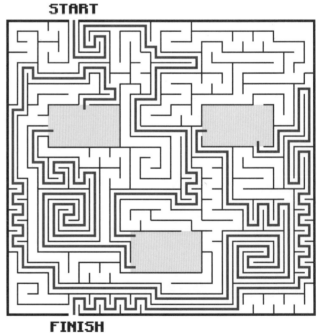

FINDERS KEEPERS (Page 53)

Ben - Diamonds
Jake - Rubies
Bella - Emeralds
Jayda - Iron ore